SIMPLY THE BEST

Simply the Best

Illustrated by Anthony Lewis

Hodder
Children's
Books

a division of Hodder Headline plc

First published in Great Britain in 1996
by Hodder Children's Books

10 9 8 7 6 5 4 3 2 1

A Catalogue record for this book is available from the
British Library

ISBN 0-340-65615-8

Typeset by Avon Dataset Ltd, Bidford-on-Avon, Warks

Printed and bound in Great Britain by
Cox & Wyman Ltd, Reading, Berks

Hodder Children's Books
a division of Hodder Headline plc
338 Euston Road
London NW1 3BH

Contents

Foreword

Members of the Federation of Children's Book Groups (mainly parents) work nationally and locally to help more children discover the pleasures of books and reading. Twenty years ago I launched National Tell a Story Week as one part of this. It was a simple idea: for years Federation groups had been reading and telling stories in public places; I asked them to co-ordinate their activities in a national celebration of Story and its enduring importance in all our lives. Over the years we have had stories on boats, trains and buses, in schools and shopping precincts, in theatres, television studios and zoos, on picnics and at parties. Each year Federation members blow up countless balloons; cope with crises and disappointments as careful planning foes awry; get generally exhausted. By they do it again, and persuade others outside the Federation to join in, because each year the magic works and there is the unforgettable sight of children held voluntarily captive by the power of a story.

In all its activities the Federation had reached out

to make common cause with publishers, booksellers, teachers, librarians – anyone or any agency committed to children, books and reading. So it is very appropriate that the stories in this anthology, published to mark National Tell a Story Week's twentieth anniversary, should be chosen by some of its many friends and supporters. The stories in this collection are intriguing, funny, puzzling, surprising, challenging. They are all very different, but they all hold the attention and keep readers and listeners talking, questioning, pondering long after each ending. They are, in short, the sort of stories that turn children into readers in the fullest sense.

Pat Triggs
Past Chair, Federation of Children's Book Groups
Originator, National Tell a Story Week

The Winter Sleepwalker

Joan Aiken

Chosen by Kate Agnew, Manager,
Heffers Children's Bookshop, Cambridge

There was a man called Bernard, a miller, who lived in his water-mill on the side of the Southern Mountains, just where the forests begin to climb up the steep slopes. Bernard was a rich man because his mill, built by a rushing mountain stream, was always at work, with the water pouring down and turning its great paddle wheel. Up above the water-mill was a saw-mill and down below there was a village, with houses, church, forge, and pub.

Every day Bernard ground huge heaps of corn and wheat for the farmers who lived round about, and they paid him well. In fact, he had so much money saved up that he could have stopped working and spent his days fishing or playing the flute or walking in the woods. But he did not want to do any of those things.

What Bernard loved to do best was make carvings out of wood. Some of them were big, some were tiny. He could carve figures of men, plants, animals, angels, fish, snakes, demons, or stars. Whenever he had a spare minute from his mill work, he would take up a piece of wood and start to whittle at it with his knife. His carvings had grown famous all over the country. People bought them to decorate houses, furniture, village halls, and barons' castles.

There were no trees growing anywhere near the mill, for Bernard had cut them all down, long ago, to carve their branches into cats and dogs and mermaids and monkeys.

Bernard had a daughter, Alyss, who was very beautiful. She had gold-brown hair, and bright, sparkling eyes. She had made herself a red dress, red shoes, and red cloak. When she walked in the forest, wearing these things, she looked like a blazing fire moving along among the trees.

Dozens of men in the village wanted to marry Alyss, but she said no to every one of them.

Bernard was very proud of her beauty. 'She is fit to marry a great lord,' he often said. 'I wouldn't want her to be the wife of a local lad. What do they know! They are dull, simple bumpkins. They have not seen the world. They are as thick as planks. They are not fit for my Alyss.'

So people said, in the country round about, that Alyss was a vain, proud girl, who thought herself better than her neighbours.

In fact this was not true. Alyss never thought about her neighbours at all. She was not proud, but she had not yet met any man that she wished to marry. 'He is nice-looking, but I don't love him,' she said of Mark Smith. 'He is clever, but I don't love him,' she said of Paul Taylor. 'He is good-natured, but I don't love him,' she said of Frank Priest. 'He is strong and willing, but I don't love him,' she said of Ted Bridge. And so it went.

Every day Alyss walked in the woods by herself,

flashing like a sunrise among the dark trees. She loved to be alone, and listen to the calls of birds, or the deer and wild pigs that grunted and snuffled, the foxes that barked in the forest.

There were bears, too, higher up the mountains, big brown bears who lived close to the high peaks, guzzling up wild honey and wild apples and wild plums all summer long, and sleeping curled up in their deep caves all through the snowy winter. Alyss did not often see a bear, for their haunts were a long way from her father's mill, but she was not at all afraid of them. She was not afraid of any wild creature. She had a little pipe, which her father had carved for her, long ago, when she was small. It was made of boxwood, very hard and white. She used to play tunes on her pipe as she wandered through the forest. And the birds replied to her music with tunes of their own, and the deer and hares stopped munching to listen.

Now one day Bernard came to his daughter looking pale and worried. He said, 'Alyss, from now on I want you to sleep out in the hay barn. I shall move your bed out there this afternoon. You can have plenty of thick woollen blankets, and a goose-feather quilt; you can have a lamp and a stone bottle filled with hot water to keep you warm.'

Alyss was puzzled.

'Why, Father? Why must I sleep in the barn?'

'Never mind! You do as I say! And never come into the mill in the morning until you hear me start the wheel turning. In fact, I shall put a lock on the door of the barn, and lock you in.'

But Alyss could not stand this idea.

'No, no, Father, please don't lock me in! Suppose the barn caught fire? I can't bear to be locked in.'

Well, she begged and prayed, until at last Bernard gave in. Instead, he handed her the barn key, and told her to be sure and lock herself in every night when she went to bed.

So, from then on, Alyss slept in the barn. Her bed stood among the piles of hay and she lay under a pile of warm woollen blankets and a goose-feather quilt. At night she heard the owls hooting and the foxes yapping, the deer and the badgers grunting, the otters playing and splashing in the stream. Indeed, she was happy to sleep in the barn. Often she got up, long before it was light, and went out to wander in the forest.

As for all the men who wanted to marry her, she

never gave them a single thought. But she did wonder, sometimes, why her father had sent her out to sleep in the barn, as if she were in disgrace.

Now the reason why Bernard sent his daughter Alyss to sleep in the barn was this: a huge oak tree grew further down the valley, two miles on past the village, at a crossroads. For a long time, Bernard had his eye on this tree. He longed to cut it down, to give him a new store of wood for his carvings.

But the tree did not belong to Bernard. It belonged to no one person. It was a landmark tree. Hundreds of years ago it had been planted on the spot where the land of one village ended and the next began. So the tree belonged to both villages, and to all the people who lived in them. And it belonged to their grandparents and their grand-children. It marked the edge of the land, so the villagers knew whose job it was to mend the road, and keep the hedges trimmed.

The tree certainly did not belong to Bernard.

Just the same, one night he went, secretly, with his sharpest axe and his biggest saw, with oxen and crowbars and a cart, and he cut the great tree down. He sliced the tree into logs, and sawed off the branches, and dragged all the wood away to his storehouse. He made a bonfire of the leaves and twigs, and left the spot bare.

Now, as Bernard's axe cut through the very core and centre of the tree, he heard a small buzzing voice in his ear – a voice that sounded rather like the rasp of a saw, cutting through hard wood. The voice said: *'You have killed a tree that was not yours to kill.'*

'I wanted the wood. I needed the wood,' panted Bernard. And he went on with his chopping.

'Very well!' said the voice. 'Wood you wanted, and wood you shall have – even more wood than you asked for. Every morning when you wake from sleep, the first thing that you touch with your hand – that thing will turn into wood. And wood it will be for ever more. And much good may it do you.'

Sure enough, next morning, as soon as Bernard woke up and opened his eyes, his favourite tabby cat jumped up beside him on the bed. Bernard stretched out a hand to stroke the cat, and, straight away, the cat turned to solid wood, still and silent. It looked like a beautifully carved cat, one that Bernard might easily have made himself.

At that, a deadly cold fear came sliding into his heart.

Suppose, by mistake, he should touch his daughter Alyss?

So that was why he made her go and sleep in the barn.

The people who lived in the villages were furious that their landmark oak tree had been cut down, and they guessed at once who had done it. But done was done; the tree could not be put back. Bernard promised to plant a new young oak tree on the same spot, he gave them fine carvings to put in their churches, and after a while the matter was forgotten. But not by Bernard. He had to train himself to be very, very careful what he touched when he woke up each day. And even so, all sorts of things were turned into wood by mistake – he had a wooden teapot, wooden toothbrush, a pair of wooden trousers, a wooden lamp, a box full of wooden bars of soap, and dozens of wooden sheets and blankets.

'What very queer things you are carving these days, Father!' said Alyss.

Bernard grew very silent and gloomy. The neighbours never spoke to him, and Alyss did not spend much time with him, because he never talked to her.

She passed nearly all her days in the woods.

Autumn came. The leaves fell from the trees. A sprinkle of snow covered the ground. The squirrels buried their nuts and curled up in hollow trees for their winter nap. The bears went into their caves and curled up even tighter for a deep, deep winter sleep.

Alyss loved the winter, when dead leaves rustled on the ground, and then the snow made a white carpet, and the shapes of the trees were bare and beautiful.

She walked when it was light, she walked when it was dark. Her eyes were so used to the outdoors that she could see very well, even in the blackest night, even when there was no moon. Bernard had no idea how often she went out at night, up to the saw-mill, or down past the village, or far away into the deep forest.

One starry night, near the saw-mill, where the piles of sawdust were silent and frosty, for the woodmen were all far away, fast asleep in their beds, Alyss saw a strange thing.

A great dark shape was drifting slowly along,

making not the least sound of footsteps on the bare, icy ground.

As it came closer, Alyss could see that it was a huge brown bear.

And this surprised her very much, for, at this time of year, all the bears ought to be sound asleep, snoring in their cosy caves.

As the bear came closer, Alyss realised that it *was* fast asleep. Its eyes were shut. It drifted along softly and silently as a piece of thistledown. It even snored a little.

The bear was walking in its sleep.

Alyss said – very gently, so as not to startle it – 'Dear bear, you should be back in your cave, not on the gad out here in the freezing forest! Turn around, turn around, and go back home!'

At that, the bear stopped, and stood with its great pad-paws dangling, as if it listened to her.

'Dear bear, go home!' whispered Alyss again. Then she took her little boxwood pipe from the pocket of her red cloak, and played a soft, peaceful tune, a lullaby. The sleeping bear cocked his head to listen, then, after a minute or two, turned his great furry body, and wandered back the way he had come.

Just then, Alyss remembered something. Her mother had once told her that if you meet a person who is walking in his sleep, and ask him a question, he will always give you a true answer. So she called softly after the slowly walking bear 'Oh, bear! If you know – please tell me the name of the person I shall marry?'

The bear paused a little at that, but then slowly shook his great brown pointed head, and went drifting silently on his way.

And Alyss went slowly back to her own bed among the hay.

After that, for many nights, if the moon shone very brightly, or the stars were out, Alyss would go into the forest, and find the sleep-walking bear on the move among the trees.

Sometimes she walked along beside the bear, and played on her little boxwood pipe. And he seemed to listen for he nodded his great head slowly up and down. Sometimes, if the night was not too cold, they would find a sheltered place among the moss and leaves, under some great evergreen tree, and the bear would lay his drowsy head in her lap while she played and softly sang to him.

And, each time, as she sent him home to his cave, she would ask the same question: 'Dear bear, if you know, tell me whom shall I marry?'

But he always shook his head as he wandered away.

Almost every day men came from the village, and from other villages, farther away, asking Bernard the miller for leave to marry his daughter. But she would take none of them.

And Bernard, these days even more silent and gloomy, always had the same answer for the suitors.

'My daughter can choose whom she pleases. She is beautiful enough, and rich enough, to marry a knight or a prince or some great lord.'

But one morning, when Alyss had been wandering in the woods all night long with her friend the bear, she saw the mill door open, and her father come yawning from his bed. And she ran to him and knelt, clasping her hands round his waist, and cried out, 'Father, Father, I want to marry the bear, the sleep-walking bear from the forest!'

And as she spoke the word *forest,* her lips turned to wood. Her fingers turned to wood, her hands, her arms were wooden. Her legs and feet were wooden. She had turned into a wooden statue, but one more beautiful than Bernard could have carved, even if he had spent his whole life on the job.

The poor man felt as if he had turned to wood himself.

He did not bother to start the mill-wheel working. All that day he sat in his old wooden chair, staring at his wooden daughter. He looked down at her upturned pleading face, at her outstretched hands.

That night Bernard went out into the forest. For many hours he strode about, hunting and searching. At last, tired and grief-stricken, he lay down under a pine tree and fell into a light sleep, full of sad dreams. But at dawn, cold and stiff, he woke up, and found a great brown shape standing not far off, turning its head this way and that, as if it, too, were searching for some lost thing.

It was a bear. It was fast asleep.

Bernard walked up to the bear and laid his hand gently on one of its huge, clawed front paws. And straight away, it was changed to wood, a massive wooden statue of a bear.

Bernard brought out his ox-waggon. He lifted the two wooden creatures, the bear and the girl, on to the cart. He took them a long way up the mountain, and put them in a cave, buried in a deep bank of dead leaves, and he blocked the cave entrance with a huge stone.

Then Bernard went away, no one knew where.

The mill stands empty now, and the mill-wheel has stopped turning, and all the wooden carvings are covered with dust.

The Tunnel

Robert Swindells

Chosen by Sonia Benster, Proprietor,
The Children's Bookshop, Huddersfield

It was Renee who found it. Three weeks into the summer holidays and stuck for something to do, we'd strayed some distance beyond the boundaries of our usual territory and were investigating a stretch of scrubby land, all humps and hollows, which might once have been a quarrying area.

'Hey, you lot, come over here!'

We converged on Renee, and found her gazing at

a hole in the side of a grassy bank. It was two feet wide and two feet high, and round except that its floor was flattened a bit. It looked very old, and seemed to be made of brick.

'It's a cave,' said Mick.

'Is it heck!' scoffed Kath. 'Caves aren't made of brick.'

'What is it then, clever-clogs?'

'I don't know, do I? But it's not a cave.'

Don squatted and peered inside.

'Wonder where it goes?'

'Fairyland,' growled Georgy, who was in a mood.

'Why don't we go in and find out?' suggested Renee.

We tried it, but a few yards in we had to give it up. The light from the entrance had faded. Inky blackness lay ahead. Renee, who was leading, said, 'I can't see a thing. We could fall down a hole or something. What we need is a torch or some candles.'

We didn't have anything like that, but we'd become really interested in this tunnel so we decided to go home, scrounge whatever we could in the way of candles, matches and so on, and come back.

A torch would have been best, but nobody managed one. We ended up with two candles, some stubs and a box of matches. With these, we hurried back to the tunnel, lit up, and crawled inside.

It wasn't a pleasant experience. The floor was muddy and there was a bad smell. A sort of white mould grew downwards from the roof and our heads brushed against this, dislodging it in strands and clumps which clung to our hair. When we stopped for a breather we heard furtive, scampering sounds and here and there we saw rat droppings. The tunnel was uncomfortably narrow, and I worried that if we failed to reach the end, it might not be all that easy to turn round. I don't think any of us was really enjoying ourselves, but we felt we were having an adventure and anything was better than boredom.

We'd been crawling for an hour, and must have been something like a mile from our starting point, when Renee called, 'Hey – there's a hole in the roof here. I'm going to see if I can stand up.'

We stopped. I was in fourth position behind Renee, Don and Mick. All I could see was Mick's backside and our shadows moving on the glistening walls.

Behind me, Kath said, 'What's happening?'

I told her, and she relayed the information to Georgy, bringing up the rear.

The hole which Renee had found turned out to be quite large enough for us all to stand up in, and when we did so we found ourselves in the basement of what might have been a mill or warehouse. Bits of broken machinery, veiled in cobwebs, lay around, and there were stacks of damp, yellowing paper. We'd have liked to explore, but we were scared to. What if somebody came down and caught us, and we said we'd come through the sewer? Was that trespassing? Breaking and entering? Would we end up in jail? Anyway, we contented ourselves with sitting round the hole, dangling our legs and talking in whispers. We'd doused the candles to save them, and in case anybody saw the light, and we sat in the pitch blackness for ten or fifteen minutes, exercising our jaws and giving our bruised knees a rest.

Presently Renee said, 'How about moving on now?' and we lowered ourselves into the tunnel in the same order as before.

We didn't go much farther. Our candles were burning low. We were cold and tired and there was no sign that the tunnel might be coming to an end. We paused long enough to scrawl a message in candle wax on the wall.

'WE WERE HERE' it said. '16/8/51.'

We would have signed our names, but we daren't waste any more wax.

It seemed a long way back. When we finally emerged it was twilight and we were down to our last stump of candle. We felt great. At last we'd had a real adventure, like the kids we read about in books. We climbed the bank and stood, trying to see where we'd been. Was that the building whose basement we'd been in? Or was it that one over there?

Georgy was over his mood. 'I vote we come again with torches,' he said, 'and find the other end, however far it is.'

We all thought it was a good plan, and so it was agreed.

Some of us were going away on holiday, and it was two weeks before we were able to mount our second expedition. We had torches this time and Kath even brought a spare battery, so we were well-equipped.

It never happened though, because when we got

to the place a horrifying sight met our eyes. Water was gushing in a dirty brown torrent from the mouth of the tunnel into what had been a dry stream bed and swirling away, foam-flecked, round the foot of the bank. The water, moving with great force, filled the tunnel from floor to ceiling and roared as it emerged. We didn't know where it was coming from but we knew that if it had come two weeks earlier, or half an hour later, we'd all have died.

We stood for a while, watching the water. We didn't speak. I suppose each of us was trying to imagine what it would be like, drowning in the dark. I know I was. And I shuddered, and looked at the sun, and knew it was better to be bored than dead.

The Were Puppy (Chapter Four)

Jacqueline Wilson

Chosen by Sue Bates, Past National Chairman of the Federation of Children's Book Groups

'Please, Mum,' Micky begged. 'I can't go in there!'

Mum wouldn't listen. She made Micky get out of the car.

She knocked on the front door of the dogs' home. The howling increased, and then there was a lot of barking too. Micky clung to Mum's arm, and even Marigold took a step backwards. The door opened and a young freckled woman in jeans stood there smiling, surrounded by two barking Labradors, the colour of clotted cream, and a small black Scottie who kept diving through the Labradors' legs.

'Quiet, you silly dogs,' the woman shouted. She saw Micky shrinking away and said quickly, 'It's OK, they're all very friendly. They won't bite. There's no need to be frightened of them.'

'*I'm* not frightened,' said Marigold, squatting down to pet the Scottie, while the two Labradors sniffed and nuzzled. 'Aren't they lovely? What are their names? Shall we have the little Scottie dog, Mum? Although I like the big creamy dogs too. Oh look, this one's *smiling* at me.'

'That's Tumble. And that's her brother Rough.'

'Oh great. We're a sister and brother and we can *have* a sister dog and brother dog.'

'No, I'm afraid Rough and Tumble are my dogs. And wee Jeannie here. But there are plenty of other lovely dogs to choose from out the back. I've got lots of strays at the moment. Come through to the kennels.'

'I'll wait outside,' Micky hissed, trying to dodge Rough and Tumble's big wet licks.

'Don't be silly, Micky,' said Mum. 'This is going

to be your dog. You've got to choose.'

'I'll choose for him,' said Marigold, still playing with Jeannie. She rolled over and let Marigold tickle her tummy. 'There, look! She loves being tickled, doesn't she? It's my magic trick of taming all dogs. Maybe I'll be a dog trainer in a circus as well as a bare-back rider.'

'I think it's a trick that only works with little friendly dogs like Jeannie,' said Miss Webb. 'You shouldn't even touch some of the big dogs I've got out the back, just in case.'

'I'm not scared of any dogs, even really big ones,' Marigold boasted. 'Not like my brother. He's older than me too, and yet he's *ever* so scared.'

'No I'm not,' Micky said hoarsely, but at that moment Jeannie nudged against his leg and he gave a little yelp of terror.

'See that!' said Marigold triumphantly. 'He's even scared of a little Scottie. He's hopeless, isn't he? I don't know why Mum wants to get him a dog, it's just daft, isn't it? She ought to get me a dog, seeing as I'm the one that likes them. And dogs don't need a special stable, do they? Just a little kennel.'

'Or even an old cardboard box,' said Miss Webb.

'I've got special big kennels at the back of my house because I always have so many stray dogs on my hands.' She turned back to Micky. 'But it's OK, they're all in separate pens and they can't get out.'

'He'll still be scared,' said Marigold. 'He's even scared of me.' She suddenly darted at Micky, going woof-woof-woof and poor Micky was so strung up and startled by this time that he jumped and very nearly burst into tears.

'Marigold!' said Mum, but she gave Micky a shake too, obviously embarrassed.

Marigold just laughed and Miss Webb was trying hard to keep a straight face. Micky blinked desperately, and tried to swallow the lump in his throat. His face was scarlet, his whole body burning.

'We've got some puppies out the back,' said Miss Webb. 'They're really sweet and cuddly. I'd have a puppy if I were you.'

Micky's throat ached so much he could barely speak.

'I don't really want any dog. Not even a puppy, thank you,' he croaked.

'Just take a look, Micky,' said Mum, giving him a little push.

So Micky had to go with them to the kennels at the back of the house. The howling got louder. It had a strange eerie edge to it. Marigold put her hands over her ears.

'Which one's making that horrid noise?' she complained.

'Yes, sorry. That's a stray we picked up last night. He's been making that row ever since, though we've done our best to comfort him. He's only a puppy, but he's a vicious little thing all the same. I certainly wouldn't recommend him for a family pet, especially as the little boy's so nervous.'

'I bet I could tame him,' Marigold boasted. She approached the pen in the corner, where a big grey puppy stood tensely, head back, howling horribly.

'Nice doggie,' said Marigold, and the puppy quivered and then stopped in mid-howl.

'See that!' said Marigold excitedly. 'There, I've stopped him. He's coming over to see me. Here, boy. You like me, don't you? Do you want to be my doggie, eh? You can't be Micky's dog because he's such a silly little wet wimp.'

Micky couldn't stand the word wimp. It sounded so horrible and feeble and ugly and pimply.

'Don't call Micky silly names,' said Mum.

'Well, it's true. He really is a wimp. Even Dad says so,' said Marigold, reaching through the bars to pat the strange grey puppy. 'Dad says I should have been his boy because I've got all the spark, while Micky's just a wimp.'

Micky burned all over. He shut his eyes, his whole skin prickling, itching unbearably. He could still hear the howling but now it seemed to be right inside his own head. He ground his teeth . . . and then suddenly Marigold screamed.

Micky opened his eyes. He stared at his shrieking sister. The grey puppy had a fierce grip of her finger and was biting hard with his little razor teeth.

'Get it off me! Help, help! Oh, Mum, help, it hurts!' Marigold yelled.

A very naughty little grin bared Micky's teeth – almost as if he was biting too. Then he shook his head and Marigold managed to snatch her finger away from the savage little pup.

'*Bad* boy,' said Miss Webb to the excited puppy. 'I'm so sorry he went for you, dear. Mind you, I did try to warn you. You mustn't ever take silly risks with stray dogs. Let's have a look at that finger and see what damage has been done.'

'It's bleeding!' Marigold screamed.

'Come on now, lovie, it's only a little scratch,' said Mum, giving her a cuddle.

'Still, it's better not to take any risks. We'll give it a dab of disinfectant and find you a bandage,' said Miss Webb.

She led the wailing Marigold back into the house. Mum followed, looking a little agitated.

Micky didn't follow. He stayed where he was, out by the dog pens. He took no notice of all the ordinary dogs obedient in their pens. He didn't even give the cute Labrador puppies snuggled in their basket a second glance. He only had eyes for the strange grey puppy that had bitten Marigold.

It ran towards Micky: Micky didn't back away. He didn't feel so scared. And the puppy seemed to have perked up too. He didn't howl any more. He made little friendly snuffling sounds.

'You just bit my sister,' Micky whispered.

The puppy coughed several times. It sounded almost as if he was chuckling. Micky started giggling too.

'That was bad,' Micky spluttered, his hand over his mouth so they wouldn't hear back in the house. 'But we don't care, do we?'

The puppy shook his head. He came right up against the bars of his pen, sticking out his soft pointed snout. His amber eyes were wide and trusting now.

'Are you trying to make friends?' Micky asked.

The puppy snuffled.

'Hello, puppy,' Micky said, and he reached through the bars to pat the puppy's head, though Marigold had just demonstrated that this was a very dangerous thing to do.

'But you're not going to bite me, are you?' said Micky.

The puppy twitched his nose and blinked his eyes. Micky very gently touched the coarse grey fur. His hand was trembling. The puppy quivered too, but stayed still. Micky held his breath and started stroking very softly. The puppy pressed up even closer, in spite of the hard bars. His pink tongue came out and he licked Micky's bare knee.

'We're pals, right?' Micky whispered.

The puppy licked several times.

'Hey, I'm not a lollipop,' Micky giggled, wiping at his slobbery knee.

The puppy licked harder, sharing the joke. He managed to get one paw through the bars. He held it out to Micky. Micky shook the hard little pad solemnly.

'How do you do,' said Micky. 'I'm Micky. And that silly girl you bit was my sister Marigold.'

The puppy grinned wolfishly.

'You didn't half go for her, didn't you,' said Micky, and they had another giggle together, the puppy giving little barks of glee.

'Micky! Get away from that dog!' Mum suddenly cried, rushing out of the back of the house. 'How can you be so stupid? Look what he just did to Marigold.'

'He won't bite me,' said Micky calmly.

'Do as your mum says,' said Miss Webb, returning with Marigold. Marigold was still blotched with tears and she held her bandaged finger high in the air to show it off. 'That puppy is much too unpredictable. I don't know what I'm going to do with him.'

'I'll take him as my pet,' said Micky, and the puppy stiffened and then licked him rapturously.

'Don't be silly, Micky,' said Mum, trying to pull him away.

'I'm not being silly, Mum. I want this dog,' said Micky.

'No!' Marigold protested. 'We're not having that horrible mangy nasty thing. It bites. My finger hurts and hurts. I shall maybe have to go to the hospital to get it all stitched up.'

'Marigold, I told you, it's only a scratch,' said Mum. 'Now, Micky, leave that bad puppy alone and come and look at some of the other dogs.'

'No, Mum. I want this one. Please, I must have this puppy.'

'What about these other puppies over here? They're half Labradors and they're very gentle and docile. Look at the little black one with the big eyes. He'd make a much better pet. See, he's much prettier than that puppy there,' said Miss Webb.

'I don't mind him not being pretty. I like the way he looks,' said Micky, and he had both arms through the bars now, holding the puppy tight.

'Micky, will you leave go of him?' said Mum. 'You're really the weirdest little boy. One minute you're scared stiff of all dogs and then the next you make friends with the most vicious little creature. What is it, anyway? Alsatian?'

'It's certainly mostly German Shepherd but it's got something else mixed up with it. Something very odd,' said Miss Webb.

'I know,' said Micky, nodding solemnly. 'And I want him so. Oh, Mum, please, please, please.'

'No, he's not to have him, Mum! He'll bite me again,' Marigold protested furiously.

Mum dithered between the two of them, looking helpless. Micky looked up at her, his big brown eyes glinting amber in the sunlight.

'You said it was going to be my pet. I had to choose him. And I've chosen,' said Micky.

Mum sighed. 'All right, then. You can have that one if you really must. Only I still think it's a very silly choice.'

Micky knew it was the only possible choice. He had the most magical special pet in the whole world. His very own werewolf. Well, not quite a werewolf yet. A werepuppy.

Barry the Hedgehog

Written and illustrated by Colin Thompson

Chosen by Carol Gill,
Product Group Manager, W H Smith

Across the lawn behind the old apple trees stood a wooden shed full of lawnmowers and broken deck-chairs. Inside the shed there were cobwebs and dust and the air smelt of oily rags and dried grass. There was a wooden floor that groaned and creaked when anyone walked on it, and under the floor, snuggled into the warm dry earth, lived a family of hedgehogs.

For as long as anyone could remember they had lived there, sheltered from the wind and rain in soft dark nests of grass and newspapers.

Every spring, as the days grew brighter and warmer, they woke from their long sleep. They yawned and stretched and staggered out into the twilight to spend the summer out in the garden.

But now it was winter and time to rest. The leaves had fallen in golden piles and the shady corners where the hedgehogs had lived all summer were now open to the sky. Their hearts began to beat more slowly and their eyelids grew heavy. All round the garden they stopped what they were doing and lifted their faces to the chilly air. One by one they made their way back to the warm nest below the shed, where they curled up and fell into a deep sleep full of dreams of sunshine and soft slugs.

'Come on, Barry,' said a mother hedgehog to her young son. 'Time for bed.'

'Shan't,' said Barry.

'Come on now, there's a good boy.' But he just ignored her.

Barry had been nothing but trouble since the day he'd been born. His brothers and sisters had always behaved like hedgehogs should. They snuffled noisily round the garden eating slugs and earwigs and knocking milk bottles over. Barry kept squeezing through the hedge and stealing next-door's cat food. And while everyone else slept the afternoons away under the rhubarb, Barry rolled around collecting squashed plums on his prickles.

'I'm not tired,' he said.

'Don't be silly,' said his mother. 'It's half-past October. You must be tired.'

'Well I'm not,' said Barry, jumping in a puddle. 'Anyway, I think hibernating's really silly.'

Barry's mother decided to leave him to it. When Barry got obstinate the best thing to do was to ignore him. She crawled under the shed and nuzzled into the nest. The air was filled with the smell of damp hedgehogs and a chorus of gentle snoring.

'I'll fetch him later,' she thought to herself, but in no time at all she was fast asleep.

'I'm staying awake, me,' said Barry to a sparrow, 'all winter.'

'Idiot,' said the sparrow and flew off.

Round the back of the shed was an overgrown pile of rubbish. At the bottom of the pile under brambles and old prams was a rusty kettle and it was there that Barry decided to live.

'I'm not going back under the shed with them,' he said, 'not ever.'

He collected some leaves and grass and pushed them into the kettle. He chewed up the fat worms that had been hiding under the leaves and climbed into his new home.

'This is great,' he said to himself, 'better than that rotten shed.'

A crowd of starlings was gathering in the trees. Hundreds of them sat in long lines on the branches and across the roof of the house getting ready to go on holiday. The air was muddled up with their endless chattering.

'Oi,' shouted Barry, sticking his head out of his new home, 'come and see my house.'

'It's just an old kettle,' laughed the starlings.

'I'm staying awake all winter, me,' he shouted.

'Idiot,' chorused two thousand three hundred and forty-seven starlings and flew off to warm African gardens.

'Come back here and say that,' shouted Barry when they were out of sight.

The next few weeks were great. With all his

family asleep, there was no one to tell him what to do. There was no one to tell him when to get up, no one to tell him when to sleep and no one to tell him to be quiet. He rolled on his back in the mud, spat in the pond and shouted swear words he'd heard the rabbits use.

Fat and wicked, he sat in the little clearing in front of his house surrounded by young squirrels.

'Say another one,' squeaked the squirrels.

'BOTTOMS!' shouted Barry. All the squirrels sniggered and nudged each other.

'More, more,' they demanded. 'Show us how far you can spit.'

'Children!' shouted the adult squirrels from the trees above.

'Skinny rats!' Barry shouted after them as they all ran giggling after their parents.

The long grass was full of rotten apples that drew slugs from all over the garden. Barry got so fat he could hardly get into his kettle. The last of the golden leaves fell from the trees and the days grew shorter and darker. The other birds left the garden until there were only the sparrows and blackbirds left. Even the blue-tits had gone next door to eat peanuts.

Through October the air held on to the last warmth of summer but in November it grew colder with mornings crisp and frosty. Barry was too excited with his adventures to notice the weather. When his breath came out in little clouds he climbed into his kettle and blew up the spout.

'Tea's ready,' he shouted.

'Idiot,' said a sparrow.

'You've got no sense of humour,' said Barry. 'That's your trouble.'

It wasn't until January that the adventure began to wear thin. The frost stayed all day now. Up at the empty house with no one to light the fire the windows were covered with ice like lace curtains. In the cellar the rats shivered and thought about moving to another home. The worms went deep into the ground and next-door's cat was being fed in the house.

Barry shuffled around in the leaves finding fewer and fewer slugs. He began to lose weight and as he got thinner he lost his protection against the cold. At the bottom of his spines his fleas huddled together for warmth. He snuggled deep into his kettle and for the first time since autumn thought about his mother and his brothers and sisters. A lump came to his throat but his pride wouldn't let him go and curl up next to them under the warm shed.

'I'm staying awake all winter,' he said. But it was difficult to sound convincing with chattering teeth.

By February he was very thin and had a nasty cold that refused to go away. Every time the sun came out he thought that perhaps it was spring and that the others would soon come out from under the shed but the winter still had a long way to go and to prove it, it started to snow.

It began as he fell asleep and it snowed all night. Barry curled up as small as he could in his kettle but the cold went right through him. It crept down his spines like sharp needles. His paws had turned blue and hurt so much he could hardly move them. He knew now why hedgehogs hibernate. His tears ran cold down his face, turning to ice in the straw and making him even colder. His teeth chattered and his brain began to slide into a deep sleep.

With one great effort he pulled himself out of the kettle and went to look for the tunnel under the shed. But the snow had fallen so heavily that the entrance was buried and he couldn't find it. Round and round the shed he crawled getting weaker and weaker, until the greatest idea in the whole world seemed to be to curl up and go to sleep.

Sleep was wonderful. The snow grew warm as he faded away. He dreamt he was curled up in a nest of feathers with all his brothers and sisters. Then through the warmth, dark shapes appeared. Closer and closer they came, but Barry was so comfortable in the arms of death that he didn't see them.

'Hey, wake up,' said a voice.

'Come on,' said another, pushing him with a soft foot.

'Go away,' Barry heard himself mumble, but the voices kept pushing and poking him until he opened his eyes and unrolled.

Standing over him were Dave and Ernie, the two biggest rabbits in the garden. Barry suddenly felt afraid, but they were smiling down at him.

'Come on, young fellow. You can't sleep there. You'll be dead in no time at all,' said Dave.

'I can't find the way in,' said Barry, beginning to cry again.

'That's all right,' said Ernie. 'You come home with us.'

'But—' started Barry, remembering all the

warnings his mother had given him about the rabbits.

'You'll die if you stay out here,' said Dave.

The two rabbits led the little hedgehog through the snowdrifts towards the warmth and safety of their underground home. Barry's feet were chapped and split from the cold and left little spots of blood on the snow. It seemed to take forever to reach the bottom of the garden.

As they dived down the tunnel into the rabbits' home the smell of fresh summer grass rose up to greet them. Deeper and deeper they went into the warren. On all sides of them there were more tunnels leading off into snug rooms where groups of rabbits peered out as they passed.

'Watcha got there, Ernie?' shouted a laughing voice. 'A pin-cushion?'

'Nah, he's brought Hilda a bag of nails,' called another.

At last they took a sharp turn left and came to a stop. Barry was so out of breath from keeping up with the long-legged rabbits that he couldn't speak. He certainly wasn't cold any more.

Ernie's wife Hilda and six young rabbits sat in the corner eating grass.

'Look what we found out in the snow,' said Ernie.

'Poor little mite,' said Hilda. 'He looks half-starved.'

Barry had been too cold and frightened to think about it but he realised that he hadn't eaten anything for three days.

'Here, help yourself,' said the young rabbits, offering Barry their grass.

'I've never eaten grass,' said Barry. 'I don't think hedgehogs do.'

'Well, what do they eat?' asked Ernie.

'Slugs and worms and things like that.'

'Slugs?' chorused the young rabbits, 'how revolting.'

'Well yes, children,' said Hilda. 'It may seem revolting to us but it just so happens we're up to here with slugs and they're eating us out of house and home.'

'My goodness, you're right,' said Ernie. 'Wayne, Elvis, take our guest down to the larder.'

The two rabbits led Barry down deeper into the warren until they were far out under the river bed. They came to a huge cave piled high with grass and roots and leaves. Wherever he looked Barry could see thousands upon thousands of slugs. It was like a hundred Christmas dinners and three supermarkets rolled into one.

There were slugs of every size and colour from the tiny Mauve Mouthful to the wonderful succulent Brown Breakfast. There were slugs that Barry had heard about only in stories, like the Golden Gumdrop and the shining Great White Pudding. There were slugs that he had thought existed only in fairy tales, like the exquisite Scarlet Slimebag that hedgehogs were supposed to have fought wars over. And lurking in the shadows like a vast beached whale, was the gigantically massively hugely enormous legendary Black Banquet. It rolled across the grass swallowing half a lawn a day and blowing out clouds of foul smelling steam. There seemed to be an endless variety of slugs and they were all for Barry.

The rabbits couldn't bear to watch as he dived into a pile of grass and began to eat. One by one they turned green and left the room.

'I don't know what they're so disgusted about,' thought Barry. 'At least I don't eat my food twice like they do.'

For the next three weeks Barry hardly left the larder. He ate and slept then ate some more and slept again. At first the young rabbits would hide in the tunnel giggling and daring each other to go and watch him eating but they all got used to it and he soon became friends with everyone.

'My mum and all the other animals say you're all crooks and dead common,' he said, 'but she's wrong.'

'We don't care,' said Ernie. 'Stops them bothering us.'

'She says you shout and swear all the time, but I think you're all great.'

'Well, we like to have a good time,' said Hilda.

'Rock and roll,' said Wayne.

'Yeah,' said Elvis.

March came and went and in early April Barry felt a breath of air from above ground tickle the back of his nose. Spring had arrived and was calling him.

Below the shed the other hedgehogs began to stir. Barry's mother rolled over and stretched. She reached out with her eyes still closed to where Barry should have been, but the grass was cold and damp. At first she thought he might have got up early, but when she looked she could see that his bed hadn't been slept in at all.

She woke the others and they hurried out into the spring sunshine. Over a winter of hibernating they had grown thin and the sunlight blinded them after their long sleep of darkness.

'He's dead,' cried Barry's mother, 'I know he is. My poor little mite is frozen stiff and all alone.'

She snuffled around in the grass and bushes but there was no sign of him. She found his kettle but it was cold and empty.

'I blame myself,' said Barry's mother, 'I should never have left him.'

She raced round and round in circles looking for her son. There was no stopping her. The others tried to tell her she was wasting her time but she didn't hear them.

She ran in larger and larger circles until she was right out of the orchard and down near the bottom of the garden. She darted under bushes, looked deep into the pond, jumped over a rotten log and came crashing down on a big fat prickly mattress.

'Hello, Mum.'

'Barry?'

'Hello, Mum.'

'Barry, is it really you?'

'Yes, Mum.'

'I thought you were dead,' said his mother, hugging him the way only one hedgehog can hug another.

They went back to the shed and while all the others sat in a big circle he told them his story. It took two days to tell it because every time he started describing the wonderful slugs he had eaten, everyone had to rush outside and find some food.

'Now then, young hedgehogs, just let that be a lesson to you all,' said a wise old grandfather.

'How do you mean, sir?' said Barry's little brother.

'Well, er, you tell them, Barry.'

'The moral of the story is that if you don't listen to your mother you could end up with lots of new friends and tons and tons of amazing slugs to eat.'

'BARRY!'

'Sorry, Mum.'

The Wreck of the Zanzibar

Michael Morpurgo

Chosen by Victoria Birkett, Buying Director, Scholastic Ltd

September 8th

Today I found a turtle. I think it's called a leatherback turtle. I found one once before, but it was dead. This one has been washed up alive.

Father had sent me down to collect drift-wood on Rushy Bay. He said there'd be plenty about after a storm like that. He was right.

I'd been there for half an hour or so heaping up

the wood, before I noticed the turtle in the tideline of piled seaweed. I thought at first he was just a washed-up tree stump covered in seaweed.

He was upside down on the sand. I pulled the seaweed off him. His eyes were open, unblinking. He was more dead than alive, I thought. His flippers were quite still, and held out to the clouds above as if he was worshipping them. He was massive, as long as this bed, and wider. He had a face like a 200 year old man, wizened and wrinkled and wise and a gently smiling mouth.

I looked around, and there were more gulls gathering. They were silent, watching, waiting; and I knew well enough what they were waiting for. I pulled away more of the seaweed and saw that the gulls had been at him already. There was blood under his neck where the skin had been pecked. I had got there just in time. I bombarded the gulls with pebbles and they flew off protesting noisily, leaving me alone with my turtle.

I knew it would be impossible to roll him over, but I tried anyway. I could rock him back and forth on his shell, but I could not turn him over, no matter how hard I tried. After a while I gave up and sat down beside him on the sand. His eyes kept closing slowly as if he was dropping off to sleep, or maybe he was dying – I couldn't be sure. I stroked him under his chin where I thought he would like it, keeping my hand well away from his mouth.

A great curling stormwave broke and came tumbling towards us. When it went hissing back over the sand, it left behind a broken spar. It was as if the sea was telling me what to do. I dragged the spar up the beach. Then I saw the turtle's head go back and his eyes closed. I've often seen seabirds like that. Once their heads go back there's nothing you can do. But I couldn't just let him die. I couldn't. I shouted at him. I shook him. I told him he wasn't to die, that I'd turn him over somehow, that it wouldn't be long.

I dug a deep hole in the sand beside him. I would lever him up and topple him in. I drove the spar into the sand underneath his shell. I drove it in again and again, until it was as deep as I could get it. I hauled back on it and felt him shift. I threw all my weight on it and at last he tumbled over into the hole, and the right way up, too. But when I scrambled over to him, his head lay limp in the sand, his eyes closed to the world. There wasn't a flicker of life about him. He was dead. I was quite sure of it now. It's silly, I know – I had only known him for a few minutes – but I felt I had lost a friend.

I made a pillow of soft sea lettuce for his head and knelt beside him. I cried till there were no more tears to cry. And then I saw the gulls were back. They knew too. I screamed at them, but they just glared at me and moved in closer.

'No!' I cried. 'No!'

I would never let them have him, never. I piled a mountain of seaweed on top of him and my driftwood on top of that. The next tide would take him away. I left him and went home.

I went back to Rushy Bay this evening, at high tide, just before nightfall, to see if my turtle was gone. He was still there. The high tide had not been high enough. The gulls were gone though, all of them. I really don't know what made me want to see his face once more. I pulled the wood and seaweed away until I could see the top of his head. As I looked it moved and lifted. He was blinking up at me. He was alive again! I could have kissed him, really I could. But I didn't quite dare.

He's still there now, all covered up against the

gulls, I hope. In the morning . . . I had to stop writing because Father just came in. He hardly ever comes in my room, so I knew at once something was wrong.

'You all right?' he said, standing in the doorway. 'What've you been up to?'

'Nothing,' I said. 'Why?'

'Old man Jenkins. He said he saw you down on Rushy Bay.'

'I was just collecting the wood,' I told him, as calmly as I could, 'like you said I should.' I find lying so difficult. I'm just not good at it.

'He thought you were crying, crying your eyes out, he says.'

'I was not,' I said, but I dared not look at him. I pretended to go on writing in my diary.

'You are telling me the truth, Laura?' He knew I wasn't, he knew it.

' 'Course,' I said. I just wished he would go.

'What do you find to write in that diary of yours?' he asked.

'Things,' I said. 'Just things.'

And he went out and shut the door behind him. He knows something, but he doesn't know what. I'm going to have to be very careful. If Father finds out about the turtle, I'm in trouble. He's only got to go down to Rushy Bay and look. That turtle would just be food to him, and to anyone else who finds him. We're all hungry, everyone is getting hungrier every day. I should tell him. I know I should. But I can't do it. I just can't let them eat him.

In the morning early, I'll have to get him back into the sea. I don't know how I'm going to do it, but somehow I will. I must. Now it's not only the gulls I have to save him from.

September 9th
The Day of the Turtle

I shall remember today as long as I live. This morning I slipped away as soon as ever I could. No one saw me go and no one followed me, I made quite sure of that. I'd lain awake most of the night wondering how I was going to get my turtle back into the water. But as I made my way to Rushy Bay, the morning fog lifting off the sea, I had no idea at all how I would do it. Even as I uncovered him, I still didn't know. I only knew it had to be done. So I talked to him. I was trying to explain it all to him, how he mustn't worry, how I'd find a way, but that I didn't yet know what way. He's got eyes that make you think he understands.

Maybe he doesn't, but you never know. Somehow, once I'd started talking, I felt it was rude not to go on. I fetched some seawater in my hat and I poured it over him. He seemed to like it, lifting his head into it as I poured. So I did it again and again. I told him all about the storm, about Granny May's roof, about the battered boats, and he looked at me. He was listening.

He was so weak though. He kept trying to move, trying to dig his flippers into the sand, but he hadn't the strength to do it. His mouth kept opening and shutting as if he was gasping for breath.

Then I had an idea. I scooped out a long deep channel all the way down to the sea. I would wait for the tide to come in as far as it could, and when the time came I would ease him down into the channel and he could wade out to sea. As I dug I told him my plan. When I'd finished I lay down beside him, exhausted, and waited for the tide.

I told him then all about Billy, about Joseph Hannibal and the General Lee, and about how I missed Billy so much, all about the cows dying and about how nothing had gone right since the day Billy left. When I looked across at him his eyes were closed. He seemed to be dozing in the sun. I'd been talking to myself.

The gulls never left us alone, not for a minute. They stood eyeing us from the rocks, from the shallows. When I threw stones at them now, they didn't fly off, they just hopped a little further away, and they always came back. I didn't go home for lunch – I just hoped Father wouldn't come looking for me. I couldn't leave my turtle, not with the gulls all around us just waiting their moment.

Besides, the tide was coming in now, closer all the time. Then there was barely five yards of sand left between the sea and my turtle, and the water was washing up the channel just as I'd planned it. It was now or never.

I told him what he had to do. 'You've got to walk the rest,' I said. 'You want to get back in the sea, you've got to walk, you hear me?'

He tried. He honestly tried. Time and again he dug the edge of his flippers into the sand, but he just couldn't move himself.

The flippers dug in again, again, but he stayed where he was. I tried pushing him from behind. That didn't work. I tried moving his flippers for him one by one. That didn't work. I slapped his shell. I shouted at him. All he did was swallow once or twice and blink at me. In the end I tried threatening him. I crouched down in front of him.

'All right,' I said. 'All right. You stay here if you like. See if I care. You see those gulls? You know what they're waiting for? If they don't get you, then someone else'll find you and you'll be turtle stew.' I was shouting at him now. I was really shouting at him. 'Turtle stew, you hear me?' All the while his eyes never left my face, not for a moment. Bullying hadn't worked either. So now I tried begging.

'Please,' I said, 'please.' But his eyes gave me the answer I already knew. He could not move. He hadn't the strength. There was nothing else left to try. From the look in his eyes I think he knew it too.

I wandered some way away from him and sat down on a rock to think. I was still thinking, fruitlessly, when I saw the gig coming around Droppy Nose Point and heading out to sea. Father was there – I recognised his cap. Old man Jenkins was in Billy's place and the Chief was setting the jibsail. They were far too far away to see my turtle. I came back to him and sat down.

'See that gig?' I told him. 'One day I'm going to row in that gig, just like Billy did. One day.'

And I told him all about the gig and the big ships that come into Scilly needing a pilot to bring them in safely, and how the gigs race each other out to get there first. I told him about the wrecks too, and about how the gigs will put to sea in any weather if there's sailors to rescue or cargo to salvage. The strange thing is, I didn't feel at all silly talking to my turtle. I mean, I know it is silly, but it just seemed the natural thing to do. I honestly think I told the turtle more about me that I've ever told anyone before.

I looked down at him. He was nudging at the sand with his chin, his mouth opening. He was hungry! I don't know why I hadn't thought of it before. I had no idea at all what turtles eat. So I tried what was nearest first – seaweed of all sorts, sea lettuce, bladderwrack, whatever I could find.

I dangled it in front of his mouth, brushing his nose with it so he could smell it. He looked as if he was going to eat it. He opened his mouth slowly and snapped at it. But then he turned his head away and let it fall to the ground.

'What then?' I asked.

A sudden shadow fell across me. Granny May was standing above me in her hat.

'How long have you been there?' I asked.

'Long enough,' she said and she walked around me to get a better look at the turtle.

'Let's try shrimps,' she said. 'Maybe he'll eat shrimps. We'd better hurry. We don't want anyone else finding him, do we?' And she sent me off home to fetch the shrimping net. I ran all the way there and all the way back, wondering if Granny May knew about her roof yet.

Granny May is the best shrimper on the island. She knows every likely cluster of seaweed on Rushy Bay, and everywhere else come to that. One sweep through the shallows and she was back, her net jumping with shrimps. She smiled down at my turtle.

'Useful, that is,' she said, tapping him with her stick.

'What?' I replied.

'Carrying your house around with you. Can't hardly have your roof blowed off, can you?' So she did know. 'It'll mend,' she said. 'Roofs you can mend easily enough, hope is a little harder.'

She told me to dig out a bowl in the sand, right under the turtle's chin, and then she shook out her net. He looked mildly interested for a moment and then looked away. It was no good. Granny May was looking out to sea, shielding her eyes against the glare of the sun.

'I wonder,' she murmured. 'I wonder. I shan't be long.' And she was gone down to the sea. She was wading out up to her ankles, then up to her knees, her shrimping net scooping through the water around her. I stayed behind with the turtle and threw more stones at the gulls. When she came back, her net was bulging with jellyfish, blue jellyfish. She emptied them into the turtle's sandy bowl. At once he was at them like a vulture, snapping, crunching, swallowing, until there wasn't a tentacle left.

'He's smiling,' she said. 'I think he likes them. I think perhaps he'd like some more.'

'I'll do it,' I said.

I picked up the net and rushed off down into the sea. They were not difficult to find. I've never liked jellyfish, not since I was stung on my neck when I was little and came out in a burning weal that lasted for months. So I kept a wary eye around me. I scooped up twelve big ones in as many minutes. He ate those and then lifted his head, asking for more. We took it in turns after that, Granny May and me, until at last he seemed to have had enough and left a half-chewed jellyfish lying there, the shrimps still hopping all around it. I crouched down and looked my turtle in the eye.

'Feel better now?' I asked, and I wondered if turtles burp when they've eaten too fast. He didn't burp, but he did move. The flippers dug deeper. He shifted – just a little at first. And then he was scooping himself slowly forward, inching his way through the sand. I went loony. I was cavorting up and down like a wild thing, and Granny May was just the same. The two of us whistled and whooped to keep him moving, but we knew soon enough that we didn't need to. Every step he took was stronger, his neck reaching forward purposefully. Nothing would stop him now. As he neared the sea, the sand was tide-rippled and wet, and he moved ever faster, faster, past the rock pools and across the muddy sand where the lugworms leave their curly casts. His flippers were under the water now. He was half walking, half swimming. Then he dipped his snout into the sea and let the water run over his head and down his neck. He was going, and suddenly I didn't want him to. I was alongside him, bending over him.

'You don't have to go,' I said.

'He wants to,' said Granny May. 'He has to.' He was in deeper water now, and with a few powerful strokes he was gone, cruising out through the turquoise water of the shallows to the deep blue beyond. The last I saw of him he was a dark shadow under the sea making out towards Samson.

I felt suddenly alone. Granny May knew it I think, because she put her arm around me and kissed the top of my head.

Back at home we never said a word about our turtle. It wasn't an arranged secret, nothing like that. We just didn't tell anyone because we didn't want to – it was private somehow.

Father says he'll try to make a start on her house tomorrow, just to keep out the weather. Granny May doesn't seem at all interested.

She just keeps smiling at me, confidentially. Mother knows something is going on between us, but she doesn't know what. I'd like to tell her, but I can't talk to her like I used to.

If Billy were here I'd tell him.

I haven't thought about Billy today and I should have. All I've thought about is my turtle. If I don't think about Billy I'll forget him, and then it'll be as if he was never here at all, as if I never had a brother, as if he never existed, and if he never existed then he can't come back, and he must. He must.

This is the longest day I've ever written in my diary and all because of a turtle. My wrist aches.

My Best Fiend (Chapter Eight)

Sheila Lavelle

Chosen by Alan Giles,

Managing Director, Waterstone's

Playing tricks on people is Angela's favourite hobby. She even does it to me sometimes, and I'm supposed to be her best friend. Once she rushed into our house shouting 'Charlie! Quick! Come and see! There's a man walking down the street with no trousers on!' I went dashing out to have a look, but it was only Mr MacLennon in his kilt, and Angela fell about laughing when she saw my face.

My dad thought it was funny too, but my mum said Angela was a very rude girl.

Angela does things like that all the time, so it's not really surprising that I thought her laryngitis was just another one of her jokes. It was a Monday morning, and when she called for me on the way to school she had her neck all muffled up in a woolly scarf. I asked her what was the matter, but she could only talk in a hoarse sort of whisper and she told me she'd lost her voice.

Well, I looked at her and all I did was laugh. I was certain it was a trick, especially after what had happened on Friday, so I'd better tell you about that first.

That Friday had been a bad day for Angela, because she was in one of her talkative moods and you know how that always gets on teachers' nerves. My dad says that when Angela is in one of her talkative moods she's even worse than her mother. Anyway, Miss Bennett had to keep on telling her to shut up all day long, and by the last lesson, which was Nature Study, everybody was getting a bit fed up.

We were doing the Life History of the Frog, and the trouble was that Angela knew it all already. In fact the whole class knew it all already because we'd done the Life History of the Frog last year in Mrs Moody's class and the year before in Miss Whiteman's *and* the year before that in Miss Spender's, and it seems to me that you have to do the Life History of the Frog in every class in every school from the Kindergarten to the Sixth Form. Teachers get ever so flustered and upset if you say you've done it before so you have to let them get on with it and pretend it's all new and interesting. But I don't mind doing it all over again because I like drawing those funny little tadpoles with their wiggly tails and I'm getting quite good at them now.

Anyway, Miss Bennett had some baby tadpoles in a jar and she was holding them up in front of the class while she talked so that we could all see them.

'And then, after the eggs hatch out,' she said, 'the tadpoles feed on the jelly around them.'

Angela bobbed up out of her chair. 'Please, Miss Bennett,' she said. 'I saw this programme on the telly the other day. And the man said they don't think that's true any more. Everybody used to think so but now they've found out that the jelly is only a sort of protection, and the baby tadpoles feed on pondweed and possibly small organisations in the water.'

Miss Bennett sighed. 'I think you mean organisms, Angela,' she said. Angela nodded and sat down.

'Well, that's most interesting,' continued Miss Bennett. 'You can see how science is discovering new facts all the time. Now, where was I? Oh, yes. The young tadpoles breathe under water by means of—'

'Gills,' said Angela, bouncing out of her desk again. 'They're very interesting things, Miss Bennett, because they can absorb oxygen from the water.'

Miss Bennett frowned. 'That's quite correct, Angela,' she said. 'I'm glad you know so much about it. But I'd rather you didn't interrupt the lesson. There'll be plenty of time for discussion afterwards.' Miss Bennett looked down at the jar of tadpoles.

'Now, the hind legs develop first, and then the—'

But Angela was on her feet again. 'I'm sorry, Miss Bennett,' she said. 'But the man on the telly said that all the legs develop at the same time. It only looks as if the hind legs develop first, because the front ones are hidden by the gill flaps.'

'Angela!' said Miss Bennett crossly. 'I have asked you not to interrupt. If it happens again I shall have to send you out of the room. I don't know what's the matter with you today.' Miss Bennett started to walk around the room, stopping at each desk to show us the tadpoles in the jar.

'This is the stage these tadpoles are at now,' she went on. 'They are growing very rapidly and need lots of food. We can even give them small pieces of meat to nibble and—'

'Excuse me, Miss Bennett,' said Angela, jumping up yet again. 'But when we were in Miss Spender's class, Miss Spender said . . .'

Miss Bennett slammed the jar of tadpoles down on my desk with such a crash that some of the water slopped over the top. I watched the tadpoles wriggling with fright and I knew just how they felt.

'Angela Mitchell!' snapped Miss Bennett. 'I don't want to hear one more word from you today. You will please stand outside the door for the remainder of the lesson. And when you go home you will write out fifty times, "I must not speak until I'm spoken to" and bring it to me on Monday morning.'

I could tell by Angela's face that she was furious. Her mouth went all sulky and she stalked out of the room. I even thought she was going to slam the door, but there are some things that even Angela daren't do. She was still furious when school finished for the day and we started walking home together.

'That Miss Bennett is an old cat,' she muttered, with a scowl. 'I'm never going to speak to her again. Not ever!'

'Oh, Angela,' I said. 'You don't really mean that.'

Angela stamped her foot in temper and pushed me away from her. 'You're pathetic,' she said. 'I most certainly do mean it. And if you were a proper sort of friend, YOU wouldn't speak to her again EITHER!'

We went home and I didn't see Angela at all on Saturday or Sunday because my mum and dad and I drove up to Newcastle that night to stay with my grandma, and she's my dad's mother and she's kind and fat and cuddly and she bakes the best stottie cakes in the North East. We didn't get back until very late on Sunday evening, so the next time

I saw Angela was on Monday morning. And that was when she came round and told me she'd lost her voice.

Well, can you blame me if I didn't believe her? I looked at her suspiciously, and she had that sparkly look in her eyes that always means she's up to something.

'You haven't really lost your voice,' I said. 'Not really and truly. It's a trick. It's just so you won't have to talk to Miss Bennett, isn't it?' But she shook her head and pointed into her mouth.

'Laryngitis,' she whispered, and gave a husky sort of giggle, and I started to giggle too. I thought it was the funniest joke she had ever thought of, and I couldn't wait to see what happened when she tried it out on Miss Bennett.

So off we went to school and the first thing Miss Bennett said when we went into the classroom after prayers was 'Well, Angela? Did you do your lines?'

Angela smiled politely and nodded her head. She opened her satchel and put some sheets of paper on Miss Bennett's desk.

'Thank you, Angela,' said Miss Bennett. 'I hope this has taught you a lesson. We'll say no more about it, but I would like you to promise that it won't happen again.'

Angela opened and shut her mouth once or twice and made a funny little croaking sound. I had to stuff my hanky in my mouth to stop myself from laughing when she solemnly shook her head and pointed her finger down her throat.

'Can't . . .' she whispered, 'can't talk.'

'Oh, dear,' said Miss Bennett. 'What's the matter, Angela? Have you lost your voice or something?' Angela nodded hard and Miss Bennett gave her a sympathetic little smile.

'Well, I'm sorry to hear that,' she said. 'But at least it means we'll all get some peace and quiet for a couple of days.' Everybody laughed when Miss Bennett said that, because it was a joke, and you always have to laugh at teachers' jokes. Angela went to her seat, blushing and scowling, and I heard Laurence Parker hiss 'Dummy!' at her as she went past.

'And now let's get on with our poetry lesson,' said Miss Bennett. 'We've wasted enough time this morning. I hope you've learnt your poem over the weekend. Charlotte, will you please stand up and recite the first few lines of Wordsworth's "Daffodils".'

I got up and took a quick peep over my shoulder at Angela. And then I suddenly went cold all over because she was staring at me in a funny sort of way and telling me something with her eyes. I knew what she wanted me to do. She wanted me to prove that I was a proper sort of friend. She wanted me to pretend that I'd lost my voice too, so that I wouldn't have to speak to Miss Bennett either.

'Well, come along, Charlotte,' said Miss Bennett impatiently. 'You haven't forgotten it, surely?'

I gazed miserably down at my desk and thought if Angela was brave enough to do it then I must be too, or she would never forgive me. She would choose somebody else to be her best friend and it would probably be that awful Delilah Jones. I opened my mouth.

'I wandered lonely . . .' I whispered, and then stopped.

Miss Bennett stared at me suspiciously.

'What's the matter?' she said in a stern voice.

I pointed down my throat and shook my head, just as Angela had done. Miss Bennett looked from me to Angela and then back again.

'Charlotte Ellis!' she said sharply. 'This is quite

ridiculous! You can't mean that you've lost your voice, too?' I nodded dumbly and Miss Bennett's face went pink and some of the boys started to snigger.

'I'm afraid I find this very hard to believe,' said Miss Bennett icily. 'That you should both happen to lose your voices on the same day. I don't suppose either of you has a note from your doctor?'

I shook my head again and looked at Angela, expecting her to do the same. Now we're for it, I thought. But Angela was rummaging in her satchel and then I couldn't believe my eyes because she got out a small white envelope and took it to Miss Bennett with a polite smile. My heart sank into a big heavy lump at the bottom of my stomach.

Miss Bennett opened the envelope and read the note

'This is indeed from Angela's doctor,' she said. 'It explains that Angela has a mild throat ailment and has lost her voice. It says that it is not serious or infectious, however, and she is quite well enough to attend school providing she stays indoors at break times.' Miss Bennett folded the note and glared at me over the top of her glasses.

'Well, Charlotte? I suppose you have a note from your doctor?'

I swallowed and croaked weakly, 'No, Miss Bennett.'

'And in fact you haven't lost your voice at all,' said Miss Bennett in an ominous sort of way.

I hung my head. 'No, Miss Bennett,' I said.

'Then what is your explanation for this strange behaviour?'

'It was . . . it was a joke,' I mumbled. Everybody tittered and giggled and Miss Bennett looked round the room with a stern expression.

'I'm afraid none of us find that sort of joke in the least amusing, do we?' she said to the class. And they all stopped sniggering and shook their heads solemnly, and doesn't it make you sick the way everybody always agrees with the teacher?

'Charlotte, you will stay indoors at break time and clean out the art cupboard as a punishment,' said Miss Bennett. 'And you will please try to behave more sensibly in future.'

'Yes, Miss Bennett. Thank you, Miss Bennett,' I breathed gratefully. Cleaning out the art cupboard is a horrible mucky job and it makes your hands all filthy but it's a lot better than some of the punishments Miss Bennett manages to think up. So I felt I was quite lucky really and I didn't mind too much when everybody else trooped out to play at the end of the lesson. Anyway, it meant that I could stay indoors with Angela, and do you know, she didn't laugh a bit about me making such a right idiot of myself about the laryngitis, and she even started to help me tidy the cupboard. But that was when the other awful thing happened.

I was clearing out all the junk which had been shoved to the back of the cupboard when I came across an old battered tin. I heaved it out and looked at the label and it said Cow Gum. I laughed and showed it to Angela.

'I wonder if that's for sticking cows,' I said. Then I started to put it away again on one of the shelves but Angela leaned over and took it out of my hands. Her face had sort of lighted up and I could see that she'd had one of her wicked ideas.

'What are you doing?' I said anxiously. Angela found a stick and prised off the lid of the tin and we both looked inside. A thick layer of glue lay at the bottom, all sticky and shiny like varnish. Angela gazed at it for a minute, then she skipped away across the room with the tin in her hands.

She stopped beside Miss Bennett's chair and started to dip the stick in the glue. I gave a shriek of horror.

'Angela! Don't!' I pleaded. 'Not Miss Bennett's chair!'

Angela turned and waved the stick at me, 'You're right,' she whispered hoarsely. 'I think I'll use it on a pig, instead.' She crossed the room quickly, and before I could even try to stop her she had scraped out a big dollop of glue and spread it all over the seat of Laurence Parker's chair.

She pushed the tin of glue back in the cupboard just in time because at that moment the bell rang for the end of break and the other children started to come back into the classroom. That nosy Delilah Jones began to wrinkle her face and sniff as soon as she came into the room.

'What's that funny smell?' she asked. But Angela only shrugged her shoulders and looked blank, and I turned my back and went on putting all the stuff back in the cupboard. I didn't know what else to do.

When I had finished I went back to my place and sat down. I had a quick peep at Laurence Parker's chair and you couldn't tell there was glue on it at all. It only looked a bit more shiny than usual. Then I saw Laurence Parker come into the room so I put my head inside my desk because I just couldn't bear to watch him sit down.

I knew Miss Bennett had come in because all the chattering suddenly stopped and I heard everybody scuttling to their places.

'We're going to do some spelling now,' came Miss Bennett's voice. 'Take out your green spelling books please, everybody. You may have five minutes to revise the twenty words we did last week, and then I'll test you on them.'

I grabbed my spelling book and when I put down my desk lid I saw that Laurence Parker was sitting in his place next to me and he hadn't noticed a thing. I looked over my shoulder, but Angela had her head down over her book and didn't look up.

It was all quiet for a few minutes while everybody except me practised their words and then Miss Bennett stood up.

'We'll start with the front row,' she said. 'I'll ask each of you to spell one word for me. Now, Delilah. You're first. Your word is, enough.'

And that awful Delilah Jones leaped up, looking

all smug and pleased with herself. 'E,N,O,U,G,H,' she said, and Miss Bennett smiled at her and said 'Well done,' and you should have seen Delilah Jones smirking all over her silly face.

Well, it went all the way along the front row and then all the way along the next row and then it was our row and I started to get that horrible feeling in my stomach that's called getting butterflies and I don't know why it's called getting butterflies because I think it feels more like great big creepy crawly caterpillars. And it was my turn at last and Miss Bennett said 'Pneumonia, Charlotte,' and it was the hardest word on the list and I should have known Miss Bennett would save that one for me. Of course I knew how to spell it. But how could I think straight? How could anybody think straight if they knew that it was Laurence Parker's turn next and he was sitting there glued to his seat?

I stood up quickly. 'New what?' I said stupidly, and Miss Bennett's mouth went all squeezed up at the corner as if she was sucking a lemon.

'Pneumonia,' she said again.

'Um, er, N,E,W . . .' I began and Laurence Parker gave a snigger.

'Sit down, Charlotte,' said Miss Bennett crossly. 'It's obvious you don't know it. You must write it out three times in your book and learn it for next week. Perhaps Laurence Parker can do better. Laurence? Pneumonia, please.'

There was a sort of horrible clatter as Laurence Parker got to his feet and I didn't know where to look because of course his chair was stuck firmly to the seat of his trousers and had got up with him. His face went all red and he swung around to try to see what was the matter, but that only made things worse because the legs of the chair crashed into the desk behind. Miss Bennett's face went as black as thunder and everybody stared like anything and there were a few smothered giggles but nobody dared laugh out loud.

'What on earth are you doing, boy?' snapped Miss Bennett and Laurence Parker started twisting about and trying to pull himself free but the chair was well and truly stuck.

'Laurence Parker! Come here AT ONCE!' shouted Miss Bennett. 'I will not tolerate this sort of clowning during my lessons!'

Laurence Parker hunched his shoulders and shuffled forward to the front of the class, clutching the chair to his bottom with his hands. He looked a bit like a fat old tortoise with its house on its back.

'I . . . I seem to have got stuck,' he stammered miserably, and Miss Bennett clucked and tutted and fussed. Then she put one hand on his shoulder and the other on the back of the chair and pulled.

There was a dreadful ripping noise and there stood Miss Bennett looking a bit surprised with the chair in her hand and hanging from the chair was a big piece of grey material. And there stood Laurence Parker looking even more surprised with a great big ragged hole in the seat of his trousers and you could see his blue and red striped Marks and Spencer's underwear. Everybody stared in horror and the whole room went dead quiet and all you could hear was people breathing and that was when I started to laugh.

It wouldn't have been so bad if it had been a quiet little giggle, or a subdued sort of chuckle, but it wasn't. It was a horrible loud cackle. My dad says that when I laugh I sound like an old hen laying an egg. And I always seem to laugh at the wrong time and in the wrong place and sometimes it gets me into terrible trouble but I can't help it.

Like the time at the vicar's garden party when Miss Menzies sneezed and her false teeth flew out and landed in the bowl of fruit punch. And that other time when we went to my Auntie Fiona's wedding up in Gateshead and my grandad trod on the end of the bride's long white veil as she was walking down the aisle and yanked it clean off her head and I laughed so much that I was sent out of the church and had to wait outside in the car so I missed the whole thing.

Anyway, Laurence Parker looked so funny standing there with that great hole in his trousers that if I hadn't laughed I'd have burst. My eyes streamed with tears and this time it was no use stuffing my hanky in my mouth because it only made me choke and laugh even more. And then of course when I started laughing like that it set everybody else off as well and soon the whole class was laughing like anything and you should have heard the din.

Miss Bennett started to thump on her desk with her fist and I knew I was in bad trouble because she only does that when she's really mad. And when I saw the way she was glaring at me I wished I hadn't laughed so much because of course that was what made her think it was me who had been messing about with the rotten old glue.

'There is glue on this chair,' said Miss Bennett, sort of quietly and ominously. 'And I don't have to ask who is responsible for this outrage.' Her eyes bored into me and I felt my face go scarlet. 'There were only two people left in this room at break time, and one of them has guilt written all over her face.' Miss Bennett turned to Laurence Parker, who had backed up against the wall to hide his underwear and was standing there looking daggers at me.

'Laurence,' she said, quite gently. 'You had better go and wait in the boys' changing room. I'm going to phone your mother and ask her to bring you a spare pair of trousers.' Then she turned back to me and her voice would have frozen the Sahara Desert. 'Charlotte Ellis, you will stay behind after school this afternoon. You and I must have a very serious talk.'

Well, of course I sort of hoped that Angela would stand up and confess, but I must admit I wasn't all that surprised when she didn't because I know what she's like. And I didn't get a single chance to speak to her on her own for the rest of the day, as she had to stay indoors again at lunch time because of her sore throat. So when four o'clock came everybody went home and I had to stay behind and get told off, and it was awful because Miss Bennett went on and on at me until I thought she'd never stop and all I could do was stand there and say nothing because of course she knew that it could only have been me or Angela and I couldn't tell on my friend, could I? Even if she did deserve it.

When at last she let me go and I escaped out of the school door, who should be waiting for me at the gate but Angela, and she had waited for me in the cold all that time. But when she squeezed my arm and whispered that I was the best friend in the whole world I pressed my lips tight together and walked away from her, because this time she'd gone too far and at least she could have taken a bit of the blame.

And then when I got home I suddenly felt a whole lot better, because my dad was there. And I told him all about it because I always tell my dad everything, and he said I was quite right not to tell on my friend. But he said Angela was a right little minx and it was high time I gave her the push and found myself a new best friend who wouldn't keep getting me into trouble.

I thought about that, and in the end I made up my mind that he was right. I even managed not to speak to Angela for three whole days.

But somehow life is never so much fun without her, and when she came round on the third day, looking as sorry as can be and carrying her favourite picture of George Michael as a peace offering, I couldn't help feeling glad to see her and I hadn't the heart to stay cross with her any longer.

The Keep-Fit Canaries (Chapters Three, Four and Five)

Written and illustrated by Jonathan Allen

Chosen by Fiona Waters,
Editorial Director, School Book Fairs

What's yellow and in the pink?

In an effort to make his life a little easier, Ralph had bought a wide-brimmed hat to protect himself from the worst of the seed-spitting.

As he approached the door of his flat he took a deep breath and put the hat on, tilting the brim so that it covered as much of his face as possible. Then he opened the door and edged into the room.

He was about to make his usual dive for the safety of the chair by the television, when he stopped. Something was different. The canaries hadn't spat a single seed at him since he'd entered the room. Were they ill? Cautiously he looked round, expecting a surprise attack at any moment. No, they didn't seem to be ill. There they were in their cage, grooming their feathers and daintily eating their seed, for all the world like a bunch of ordinary songbirds. The change was remarkable. Ralph was encouraged.

'Patient loving care,' he said to himself smugly. 'It works wonders.' He laughed. 'Who knows, one day soon they might even sing for me.'

With a light heart, he sat down and tucked into his sausage sandwich, relishing every seedless minute.

There were other distinct improvements in the canaries' behaviour. When Ralph fed them later that day, they didn't stand stock still and glare at him through their dark glasses like before. Instead, they hopped around and fluttered their tiny little wings. One canary gave out a tiny 'Tweet!' Ralph was delighted and shook out some more seed. The canary chirped twice.

The more seed I leave for them, he thought, the more they'll sing.

So from then on, each morning he left an enormous pile of seed in their food tray, and in return, the canaries twittered grudgingly. It was a start.

In the days that followed, Ralph watched them getting bigger and fitter.

'All that seed!' he said to himself. 'It must be good for them. What big, strong, healthy birds they are!'

And they were. They were broad in the shoulder, sleek of feather, bright-eyed and positively radiant with health. Ralph was pleased.

'This is all due to my expert treatment,' he boasted.

He was wrong, of course. If he could have seen what went on in the canary cage when he was out at work, he would have known better. He would have discovered the real reason for their dramatic improvement and found that it had very little to do with his so-called 'expert treatment'.

For two weeks now, the canaries had been in training. Every day, all day, they were engaged in strict body-building exercises – lifting the food dish, flapping with the pole, throwing the cuttlefish and beak-wrestling, to name but a few. They only paused to sleep, and to eat staggering amounts of seed.

Under their feathers, muscles of iron and sinews of steel were forming. It was all part of Horace's inspired plan. The canaries were making themselves strong.

Here we go, here we go, here we go!

Horace looked at his flock. He had never seen such a healthy bunch of canaries. They were fit, strong and ready for anything – which was just as well, because for what Horace had in mind they would need to be. But were they strong enough? He considered for a moment, then made up his mind.

'If we're not ready now,' he said to himself, 'we never will be!'

When Horace gave the word to begin, the canaries let out a great cheer and sprang into position. Boris, Norris and Morris flew to the side of the cage and gripped one of the bars in their beaks. Doris, Clarice and Alice gripped the bar next to it. This was the moment all their training had been leading up to.

'Ready!' they cried, in muffled voices.

'On the count of three!' shouted Horace. 'One, two, THREE!'

The six canaries pulled with all their might, tugging the two bars away from each other. All those beak and neck exercises were being put to good use.

Slowly, the bars began to bend apart. The

canaries paused for breath, then gripped the bars once more.

'This time,' cried Horace, 'all the way!'

They strained and grunted and the bars bent still further.

'All right, stop!' he yelled, and they stopped.

While everyone was recovering their breath, Horace was busy dismantling the perch. He slid the wooden pole from the wire frame and dragged it over to the bars. Then he pushed one end into the gap.

'Ready!' he shouted, standing back.

'Right!' came the reply, and all the canaries, including Horace, grabbed the other end of the pole and pushed sideways as hard as they could. The perch acted like an enormous lever, and the bars bent further and further apart.

'I think we've done it!' gasped Horace, releasing his grip.

Everyone collapsed on to the floor of the cage in a heap, panting and gasping. They would have cheered if they'd had the energy.

Horace pulled the perch out of the gap and stood back. The canaries watched, holding their breath – or what there was left of it. This was an historic moment.

'A small step for canary,' said Horace solemnly, 'but a giant leap for canarykind.' Then he squeezed through the gap and out into the room.

The canaries cheered and hugged each other, not knowing whether to laugh or cry. Some of them did both. Then they too squeezed, one by one, through the gap.

'Whooeee!' yelled Doris. 'Freedom! I like it, I like it!'

'They haven't made the cage that could hold us!' shouted Morris, as he pushed through the bent bars. 'Canaries for ever!'

The canaries all cheered, and turned to help Boris out of the cage. He was the biggest and most muscular of them all, and was having a bit of trouble getting through the gap.

'Come on, you lot. Grab my wings and pull. I'm not staying here on my own!'

Norris and Morris took hold of a wing each and heaved.

'Urk!' gasped Boris. 'I'm going to be a very long and very thin canary at this rate. Ooooh! Ah! YES!'

Like a cork from a bottle, Boris shot out of the gap in the bars and cannoned into the others, knocking them flying. A laughing, flapping ball of canaries tumbled on to the table.

At that moment, Ralph came into the room. He had taken the rest of the day off work and come home for an early lunch.

'Oh no!' he cried, when he saw what was happening. 'Why are you trying to escape? I only wanted you to sing for me!'

'All right,' said Horace, 'we'll sing for you. Come on, everybody!'

The canaries burst into song.

'Here we go, here we go, here we go!' they sang, circling the room in tight formation. 'Here we go, here we go, here we go-o!'

Ralph made a wild grab at them but missed. The canaries circled the room faster and faster, still singing.

'Now!' shouted Horace, and the formation changed direction and headed straight for the window. Glass is as nothing to a super-fit canary, so with seven crashes they went straight through it as though it wasn't there, leaving what looked like seven large bullet holes, and a single yellow feather swirling in their wake.

Free as a bird, times seven

A large canary, travelling at high speed across the classroom, is guaranteed to grab your attention.

It certainly grabbed the attention of Mrs Thompson's English class. It was one of those hot, dreamy summer days, when everything seems to be half-asleep. The birds sang, the bees buzzed, and the teacher's voice droned on. The class was drifting into a state of hazy, vague daydreams, when, suddenly: *whooooosh!*

A huge canary zoomed in through the open window, whizzed three times round the teacher, shouted, 'Yahoo!' and zoomed out again.

The class gasped. The gasp was hardly out of their mouths when: *zooooom!*

Six more large canaries whooshed into the room in tight formation, did a low, fast swoop, shouted, 'Yeehaaa!' and then split off in all directions like an Air Force display team, before zooming out again.

The class sat open-mouthed in stunned silence for a second then, with one impulse, they rushed to the window.

The canaries were falling about laughing on the school's television aerial. They slapped each other on the back and giggled uncontrollably.

'This is fun!' gasped Doris, leaning on Clarice for support while, down below, children's heads stuck out of the windows at odd angles as they tried to see where the mad canaries had gone.

'I could get to enjoy this Freedom business!' said Boris. 'That was a laugh. What shall we do next?'

Horace was in a practical mood. He felt his responsibilities as leader very keenly.

'Fun it may be,' he said, 'but there's more to life than fun. There's also food! I don't know about you lot, but I'm hungry.'

'Yeah, good!' cried Boris. 'I like the sound of that!'

'Keep talking, man, you're speaking my language,' said Doris.

In a quiet, leafy square a short distance away, a small man in a trilby hat was sitting on a bench eating his sandwiches. Every now and then he reached into a paper bag on his lap and threw a handful of stale crumbs to the birds that fluttered around him.

'There you are, my little dears!' he said in a kindly voice, and raised his sandwich towards his mouth for another bite. Suddenly there was a whooshing noise, a flash of yellow, and no sandwich. He stared at his empty hand in disbelief.

Up in a nearby tree, Horace and the rest of the canaries were chuckling through mouthfuls of peanut-butter sandwich.

'What's good enough for humans is good enough for us!' declared Horace, wiping his beak. 'Stale crumbs are an insult to canarykind. We will not lower ourselves by eating such rubbish!'

'Hooray!' cheered the other canaries. 'No more birdseed!'

'No more stupid bits of smelly cuttlefish,' yelled Doris, jumping up and down on her twig.

'Three cheers for Horace!'

The canaries all cheered. Then they took off, flew once in tight formation around the square and zoomed off into the sky.

Send Three and Fourpence, We Are Going to a Dance

Jan Mark

Chosen by Lindsey Fraser,
Executive Director, Book Trust Scotland

Mike and Ruth Dixon got on well enough, but not so well that they wanted to walk home from school together. Ruth would not have minded, but Mike, who was two classes up, preferred to amble along with his friends so that he usually arrived a long while after Ruth did.

Ruth was leaning out of the kitchen window when he came in through the side gate, kicking a brick.

'I've got a message for you,' said Mike. 'From school. Miss Middleton wants you to go and see her tomorrow before assembly, and take a dead frog.'

'What's she want *me* to take a dead frog for?' said Ruth. 'She's not my teacher. I haven't got a dead frog.'

'How should I know?' Mike let himself in. 'Where's Mum?'

'Round Mrs Todd's. Did she really say a dead frog? I mean, really say it?'

'Derek told me to tell you. It's nothing to do with me.'

Ruth cried easily. She cried now. 'I bet she never. You're pulling my leg.'

'I'm not, and you'd better do it. She said it was important – Derek said – and you know what a rotten old temper she's got,' said Mike, feelingly.

'But why me? It's not fair.' Ruth leaned her head on the window-sill and wept in earnest. 'Where'm I going to find a dead frog?'

'Well, you can peel them off the road sometimes when they've been run over. They go all dry and flat, like pressed flowers,' said Mike. He did think it a trifle unreasonable to demand dead frogs from little girls, but Miss Middleton *was* unreasonable. Everyone knew that. 'You could start a pressed frog collection,' he said.

Ruth sniffed fruitily. 'What do you think Miss'll do if I don't get one?'

'She'll go barmy, that's what,' said Mike. 'She's barmy anyway,' he said. 'Nah, don't start howling again. Look, I'll go down the ponds after tea. I know there's frogs there because I saw the spawn, back at Easter.'

'But those frogs are alive. She wants a dead one.'

'I dunno. Perhaps we could get it put to sleep or something, like Mrs Todd's Tibby was. And don't tell Mum. She doesn't like me down the ponds and she won't let us have frogs indoors. Get an old box with a lid and leave it on the rockery, and I'll put old Froggo in it when I come home. *And stop crying!*'

After Mike had gone out Ruth found the box that her summer sandals had come in. She poked air holes in the top and furnished it with damp grass and a tin lid full of water. Then she left it on the rockery with a length of darning wool so that Froggo could be fastened down safely until morning. It was only possible to imagine Froggo alive; all tender and green saying croak-croak. She could not think of him dead and flat and handed over to Miss Middleton, who definitely must have gone barmy. Perhaps Mike or Derek had been wrong about the dead part. She hoped they had.

She was in the bathroom, getting ready for bed, when Mike came home. He looked round the door and stuck up his thumbs.

'Operation Frog successful. Over and out.'

'Wait. Is he . . . alive?'

'Shhh. Mum's in the hall. Yes.'

'What's he like?'

'Sort of frog-shaped. Look, I've got him; OK? I'm going down now.'

'Is he green?'

'No. More like that pork pie that went mouldy on top. Good night!'

Mike had hidden Froggo's dungeon under the front hedge, so all Ruth had to do next morning was scoop it up as she went out of the gate. Mike had left earlier with his friends, so she paused for a moment to introduce herself. She tapped quietly on the lid. 'Hello?'

There was no answering cry of croak-croak.

Perhaps he *was* dead. Ruth felt a tear coming and raised the lid a fraction at one end. There was a scrabbling noise and at the other end of the box she saw something small and alive, crouching in the grass.

'Poor Froggo,' she whispered through the air holes. 'I won't let her kill you, I promise,' and she continued on her way to school feeling brave and desperate, and ready to protect Froggo's life at the cost of her own.

The school hall was in the middle of the building and classrooms opened off it. Miss Middleton had Class 3 this year, next to the cloakroom. Ruth hung up her blazer, untied the wool from Froggo's box, and went to meet her doom. Miss Middleton was arranging little stones in an aquarium on top of the bookcase, and jerked her head when Ruth knocked, to show that she should come in.

'I got him, Miss,' said Ruth, holding out the shoe box in trembling hands.

'What, dear?' said Miss Middleton, up to her wrists in water-weed.

'Only he's not dead and I won't let you kill him!' Ruth cried, and swept off the lid with a dramatic flourish. Froggo, who must have been waiting for this, sprung out, towards Miss Middleton, landed with a clammy sound on that vulnerable place between the collar bones, and slithered down inside Miss Middleton's blouse.

Miss Middleton taught Nature Study. She was not afraid of little damp creatures, but she was not expecting Froggo. She gave a squawk of alarm and jumped backwards. The aquarium skidded in the opposite direction; took off; shattered against a desk. The contents broke over Ruth's new sandals in a tidal wave, and Lily the goldfish thrashed about in a shallow puddle on the floor. People came running with mops and dustpans. Lily Fish was taken out by the tail to recover in the cloak-room sink. Froggo was arrested while trying to leave Miss Middleton's blouse through the gap between two buttons, and put back in his box with a weight on top in case he made another dash for freedom.

Ruth, crying harder than she had ever done in her life, was sent to stand outside the head-master's room, accused of playing stupid practical jokes; and cruelty to frogs.

Sir looked rather as if he had been laughing, but it seemed unlikely, under the circumstances, and Ruth's eyes were so swollen and tear-filled that she couldn't see clearly. He gave her a few minutes to dry out and then said, 'This isn't like you, Ruth. Whatever possessed you to go throwing frogs at poor Miss Middleton? And poor frog, come to that.'

'She told me to bring her a frog,' said Ruth, staunching another tear at the injustice of it all. 'Only she wanted a dead one, and I couldn't find a dead one, and I couldn't kill Froggo. I won't kill him,' she said, remembering her vow on the way to school.

'Miss Middleton says she did not ask you to bring her a frog, or kill a frog. She thinks you've been very foolish and unkind,' said Sir, 'and I think you are not telling the truth. Now . . .'

'Mike told me to,' said Ruth.

'Your brother? Oh, come now.'

'He did. He said Miss Middleton wanted me to go to her before assembly with a dead frog and I did, only it wasn't dead and I won't!'

'Ruth! Don't grizzle. No one is going to murder your frog, but we must get this nonsense sorted out.' Sir opened his door and called to a passer-by, 'Tell Michael Dixon that I want to see him at once, in my office.'

Mike arrived, looking wary. He had heard the crash and kept out of the way, but a summons from Sir was not to be ignored.

'Come in, Michael,' said Sir. 'Now, why did you tell your sister that Miss Middleton wanted her to bring a dead frog to school?'

'It wasn't me,' said Mike. 'It was a message from Miss Middleton.'

'Miss Middleton told you?'

'No, Derek Bingham told me. She told him to tell me – I suppose,' said Mike, sulkily. He scowled at Ruth. All her fault.

'Then you'd better fetch Derek Bingham here right away. We're going to get to the bottom of this.'

Derek arrived. He too had heard the crash.

'Come in, Derek,' said Sir. 'I understand that you told Michael here some tarradiddle about his sister. You let him think it was a message from Miss Middleton, didn't you?'

'Yes, well . . .' Derek shuffled. 'Miss Middleton didn't tell *me*. She told, er, someone, and they told me.'

'Who was this someone?'

Derek turned all noble and stood up straight

and pale. 'I can't remember, Sir.'

'Don't let's have any heroics about sneaking, Derek, or I shall get very *cross*.'

Derek's nobility ebbed rapidly. 'It was Tim Hancock, Sir. He said Miss Middleton wanted Ruth Dixon to bring her a dead dog before assembly.'

'A dead *dog*?'

'Yes, Sir.'

'Didn't you think it a bit strange that Miss Middleton should ask Ruth for a dead dog, Derek?'

'I thought she must have one, Sir.'

'But why should Miss Middleton want it?'

'Well, she does do Nature Study,' said Derek.

'Go and fetch Tim,' said Sir.

Tim had been playing football on the field when the aquarium went down. He came in with an innocent smile which wilted when he saw what was waiting for him.

'Sir?'

'Would you mind repeating the message that you gave Derek yesterday afternoon?'

'I told him Miss Middleton wanted Sue Nixon to bring her a red sock before assembly,' said Tim. 'It was important.'

'Red sock? Sue Nixon?' said Sir. He was beginning to look slightly wild-eyed. 'Who's Sue Nixon? There's no one in this school called Sue Nixon.'

'I don't know any of the girls, Sir,' said Tim.

'Didn't you think a red sock was an odd thing to ask for?'

'I thought she was bats, Sir.'

'Sue Nixon?'

'No, Sir. Miss Middleton, Sir,' said truthful Tim.

Sir raised his eyebrows. 'But why did you tell Derek?'

'I couldn't find anyone else, Sir. It was late.'

'But why Derek?'

'I had to tell someone or I'd have got into trouble,' said Tim, virtuously.

'You are in trouble,' said Sir. 'Michael, ask Miss Middleton to step in here for a moment, please.'

Miss Middleton, frog-ridden, looked round the door.

'I'm sorry to bother you again,' said Sir, 'but it seems that Tim thinks you told him that one Sue Nixon was to bring you a red sock before assembly.'

'Tim!' said Miss Middleton, very shocked. 'That's a naughty fib. I never told you any such thing.'

'Oh Sir,' said Tim, 'Miss didn't tell me. It was Pauline Bates done that.'

'*Did* that. I think I see Pauline out in the hall,' said Sir. 'In the PT class. Yes? Let's have her in.'

Pauline was very small and very frightened. Sir sat her on his knee and told her not to worry. 'All we want to know,' he said, 'is what you said to Tim yesterday. About Sue Nixon and the dead dog.'

'Red sock, Sir,' said Tim.

'Sorry. Red sock. Well, Pauline?'

Pauline looked as if she might join Ruth in tears. Ruth had just realised that she was no longer involved, and was crying with relief.

'You said Miss Middleton gave you a message for Sue Nixon. What was it?'

'It wasn't Sue Nixon,' said Pauline, damply. 'It was June Nichols. It wasn't Miss Middleton, it was Miss Wimbledon.'

'There *is* no Miss Wimbledon,' said Sir. 'June Nichols, yes. I know June, but Miss Wimbledon . . . ?'

'She means Miss Wimpole, Sir,' said Tim. 'The big girls call her Wimbledon 'cause she plays tennis, Sir, in a little skirt.'

'I thought you didn't know any girls,' said Sir. 'What did Miss Wimpole say to you, Pauline?'

'She didn't,' said Pauline. 'It was Moira

Thatcher. She said to tell June Nichols to come and see Miss Whatsit before assembly and bring her bed socks.'

'Then why tell Tim?'

'I couldn't find June. June's in his class.'

'I begin to see daylight,' said Sir. 'Not much, but it's there. All right, Pauline. Go and get Moira, please.'

Moira had recently had a new brace fitted across her front teeth. It caught the light when she opened her mouth.

'Yeth, Thir?'

'Moira, take it slowly, and tell us what the message was about June Nichols.'

Moira took a deep breath and polished the brace with her tongue.

'Well, Thir, Mith Wimpole thaid to thell June to thee her before athembly with her wed fw – thw – thth—'

'Frock?' said Sir. Moira nodded gratefully. 'So why tell Pauline?'

'Pauline liveth up her thtweet, Thir.'

'No I don't,' said Pauline. 'They moved. They got a council house, up the Ridgeway.'

'All right, Moira,' said Sir. 'Just ask Miss

Wimpole if she could thp – spare me a minute of her time, please?'

If Miss Wimpole was surprised to find eight people in Sir's office, she didn't show it. As there was no longer room to get inside, she stood at the doorway and waved. Sir waved back. Mike instantly decided that Sir fancied Miss Wimpole.

'Miss Wimpole, I believe you must be the last link in the chain. Am I right in thinking that you wanted June Nichols to see you before assembly, with her red frock?'

'Why, yes,' said Miss Wimpole. 'She's dancing a solo at the end-of-term concert. I wanted her to practise, but she didn't turn up.'

'Thank you,' said Sir. 'One day, when we both have a spare hour or two, I'll tell you why she didn't turn up. As for you lot,' he said, turning to the mob round his desk, 'you seem to have been playing Chinese Whispers without knowing it. You also seem to think that the entire staff is off its head. You may be right. I don't know. Red socks, dead dogs, live frogs – we'll put your friend in the school pond, Ruth. Fetch him at break. And now, someone had better find June Nichols and deliver Miss Wimpole's message.'

'Oh, there's no point, Sir. She couldn't have come anyway,' said Ruth. 'She's got chicken-pox. She hasn't been at school for ages.'

Acknowledgements

The Federation of Children's Book Groups and Hodder Children's Books are grateful to the Authors and original publishers for permission to reproduce the stories in this collection.

The Winter Sleepwalker by Joan Aiken was first published by Jonathan Cape Ltd in *The Winter Sleepwalker*. Copyright © 1994 Joan Aiken Enterprises.

The Keep-Fit Canaries by Jonathan Allen was first published by Doubleday. Copyright © 1992 Jonathan Allen.

My Best Fiend by Sheila Lavelle was first published in 1979 by Hamish Hamilton Ltd. Copyright © 1979 Sheila Lavelle.

Send Three and Fourpence, We Are Going to a Dance by Jan Mark was first published by Corgi in *Egbert the Elephant and Other Stories*. Copyright © 1987 Jan Mark.

The Wreck of the Zanzibar by Michael Morpurgo was first published by William Heinemann Ltd. Copyright © 1994 Michael Morpurgo.

The Tunnel by Robert Swindells was first published by Hamish Hamilton Ltd in *The Go-*

Ahead Gang. Copyright © 1992 Robert Swindells.
Barry the Hedgehog by Colin Thompson was first published by Hodder Children's Books in *Sid the Mosquito*. Copyright © 1993 Colin Thompson.
The Were Puppy by Jacqueline Wilson was first published by Blackie. Copyright © 1991 Jacqueline Wilson.

FIVE MINUTES TO BED

Read about the secret of Josh's magical stones, and discover what lives under the stairs . . .
Meet the girl who frog-hops to the moon, and a sad see-through pig who just wants to be pink!

A delightful collection of twelve bedtime stories by Joan Aiken, Margaret Mahy, Joyce Dunbar and Karen Wallace to name but a few, all selected by children's book reviewer, Julia Eccleshare.

COUNTRY TALES

Elizabeth Clark

What's so special about Mrs Puffin's prize pumpkin?
How will Mrs Spriggens get her cat back from the fairies?
Can the talkative tortoise keep his mouth shut?
And what could have scared pompous old Mr T Toad?

An outstanding collection of stories drawn from the rich traditions of folk tales and legends, woven together by a world-renowned storyteller. Perfect for reading aloud, these are stories to be shared time and time again.

Another Hodder Read Alone

SQUEAKY CLEANERS IN A MUDDLE!

Vivian French and Anna Currey

No room is too messy, no house it too big for the Squeaky Cleaners, Nina, Gina and Fred!

Six noisy baby birds – and Fred's got to look after them!
It's better than cleaning Mrs Bird's nest – but can Fred keep the naughty babies under control?

SQUEAKY CLEANERS IN A HOLE!

Vivian French and Anna Currey

No room is too messy, no house it too big for the Squeaky Cleaners, Nina, Gina and Fred!

Mr Mole wants a party.
But his home is dirty, his food keeps disappearing – and he's forgotten to send the invitations!
Can the Squeaky Cleaners help him out?